Cup of Daisies

Cup Of Daisies

ARTWORK BY KENNETH WYATT
POETRY BY KENNETH WYATT

Other books by KENNETH WYATT

Published by Y-8 Publishing Co.

Leapfrog And Other Things
I Remember

Kenneth Wyatt's Western Art
Interpreted by Charles Allen

Splash of Color

Y-8 Publishing Company
310 Comanche Trail
Tulia, Texas 79088
806-995-2239

FOREWORD

In this world of rush and hurry, I believe there is a place and even a great need for poetry. In fact poetry came into being because of a need in the world . . . a need for a vitalizing strength.

You see, poetry has about everything that music does — melody, rhythm, heart-touching moments — but this too: it can come much closer to the human soul and that makes it everlasting.

I hope my work in this book will stir your memory, recreate scenes of yesteryear, tickle your sense of humor and perhaps turn your thoughts, at times, toward God.

In school the teachers told us what we **ought** to read. I trust I may have provided what you will **want** to read.

DEDICATION

Poetry is for everyone,
but I take the privilege
of dedicating this book
of poems and paintings
to my new grandsons,

Matthew and Jakob

CONTENTS

POETRY BY KENNETH WYATT

CUP OF DAISIES. 14
GIVIN' THANKS 17
BAREFOOTIN' 19
I REMEMBER CHRISTMAS EVE 20
THINGS I KNOW. 22
AN' MAMA BAKED BREAD 26
THAT FELLER, PAPA AN' ME 28
MULES. 30
CHRISTMAS DINNER 32
TO WALK ALONE 33
THE RANGER 35
OF GOD AND LOVE .36
BIG BERT 39
NAILED DOWN 43
THE STORY TELLER 44
THE CHOICE 46
MOTHER NATURE .48
HARMONICA MUSIC 50
THE WINDMILL 52
GLADNESS 54
A CHRISTMAS PRAYER 57
THE WAR 58
THE DREAM HOUSE 61
AFORE THE LAMP WAS BLOWED OUT. 62
POINT OF VIEW 67
THE CARD GAME .68
FINGER STRINGS .70
MY SON 72
THE NEW LIFE 75
THE LAY PREACHER 76

GROWIN' 79

THE CHRISTMAS STOCKING 80

OF THINGS BROKEN 83

YOU ARE MINE. 85

THE QUILTING 87

MAMA LIKED THE WILDFLOWERS 91

THE PINTO PONY AND THE SILVER SADDLE 95

THE STEEL BRONCO. 96

THE WISH BOOK 99

DOCTORIN' 101

ABOUT GRANDMOTHERS. 102

WHEN DADDY REACHED THE BIBLE DOWN 104

THE COAL OIL LAMP 107

THE YELLER DOG 111

SIGNS 112

THE FULL CIRCLE .114

HOME ON TIME 117

TALKIN' TO THE BOSS. 119

SCHOOL DAYS 120

THE CIRCUIT RIDER 122

ONCE A DAY AND TWICE ON SUNDAY 124

CONTENTS

PAINTINGS BY KENNETH WYATT

CUP OF DAISIES 13
MAMA BAKED PIE 25
THE PROPOSAL 38
MOTHER NATURE 49
NEARING HOME 56
THE DISCUSSION 66
US TWO 74
CHAPEL AT BLUE HILL 90
BUDDIES 110
DOWN THE TRAIL 116

Cup Of Daisies

Cup Of Daisies
Oil

Cup of Daisies

Today on the street in the old part of town,
I spied an ol' beggar with head hung down.

Gloom was his partner — it was plain to be seen,
And the clothes that he wore would never be clean.

Holes in the elbows, the knees, and the seat,
There were two kinds of shoes that misfit his feet.

The frown was frozen on the face that was lined,
Plus a long black rag round his eyes that were blind.

No glimmer of hope 'bout the man could I see,
Not even in the hand he reached out to me.

The old tin cup caught the sun on its rim;
Its emptiness showed that pickins were slim.

Into that cup I dropped a coin or two,
Catching a mumble of a grumpy "thank you."

That would have been all of the story that time
'Bout me and a beggar and a nickel and dime,

But fate stepped up with his bag full of tricks,
For up the street strolled a lady of six.

With face all aglow, blue eyes shining bright,
Dress all starched and ironed just right,

Ribbons reached down in circles and swirls,
A crown of daisies entwined in her curls.

Happiness abounded — in life not a care —
Her eye then touched on the beggar out there.

Young hearts melt fast, and then, so to do,
From her hair she pulled a white daisy or two.

Softly she placed them in the battered tin cup;
Instantly the old beggar's head lifted up.

Though blind in darkness, I knew he could see
That child standing there in full sympathy.

She patted the gnarled hand, not making a sound.
From the faded black rag, a tear splashed down.

They parted then — now their hearts were as one —
But the truth was clear with what had been done.

The cup rattled louder; it had a new sound.
I walked away with something I'd found.

Let me say it so you'll recall it sometime,
"The love that she gave . . . beat a nickel and dime."

Givin' Thanks

For sunshine — warmin' the ground.
For families — where love is found.
For land — the range, the farm.
For health — kept safe from harm.

For good times — both found and sought.
For clothes — stitched and bought.
For houses — where homes are.
For food — in can and jar.

For cows — cowponies too.
For friends — and friendship true.
For churches — the days of rest.
For brothers — each one the best.

For Daddy — man among men.
For neighbors — and even kin.
For Mother — and her by law.
For sisters — without a flaw.

For boys — from son to man.
For preacher — his righteous stand.
For girls — daughters of mine.
For wife — her love sublime.

For Faith — my very breath.
For Jesus — from birth to death.
For Peace — that deals with strife.
For Salvation — from death to life.

Amen.

Barefootin'
Ink Wash

Barefootin'

While bein' a boy . . . barefootin' was style,
'Cept Sundays a course, and mid-winter while.
Oh your feet got tough an' dirty sometime,
But you wiggled your toes in freedom sublime.
'Cause a boy's a boy with feet in the dirt,
And a sole so rough that stickers can't hurt.
So early in spring, I'd kick off my shoe,
An' dress barefootin' till summer was thru.

The growin' pains come when a boy spreads tall,
An' with the growin' come changes for all.
His hair must be combed an' oil-slickered down;
Can't sleep no more with Fredrick, the hound.
The voice keeps flickerin' from tenor to rough;
As for good manners . . . they's never enough.
But the change that cuts and never does mend
Is shoe wearin' time that never does end.

From patent to leather, then back once again —
Keep up with the styles, the Joneses, the trend.
But deep in the heart of a plain country kid,
A new dream arose . . . a dream that I did.
If covering the foot jes' has to be done,
I'd dress like a man and enjoy the fun,
Maybe beat the pain of a lost boyhood . . .
For the cowboy boot is pert near as good!

I Remember Christmas Eve

I remember it now and that memory won't leave
Of a perfect night on a cold Christmas Eve.
In the stove was a fire, in the corner a tree,
Mama in the choir and there by Daddy was me.
The church was plumb full, every last pew —
Women and men . . .
Kiss an' kin . . .
We'd all stay there till the evenin' was thru.

The choir sang a special, a carol it was;
Collection was taken for the orphanage cause;
The kids all performed, an' I said a verse.
(Said Daddy some later, "It could have been worse.")
Then Brother Roland stood up and gave us a look —
Quietly did tell . . .
Did it most well . . .
The old story of Christmas he'd found in that Book.

There was quiet in the room when he finished his say,
And we all felt the glory when bowin' to pray.
But in that moment when there wadn't no sound,
Spoke a little tiny voice that turned us around.
Was Charlie's little sister a wantin' to know —
She's jes' four . . .
Not no more . . .
"Is Santa a comin' afore we all go?"

The preacher jes' grinned and wunk one eye,
"I think I saw something outside the window go by.
Looked like some cows; they's pullin' a wagon."
I caught on quick and that's not just braggin'.
"Them's reindeer!" I yelled with quaverin' voice —
Plain to me . . .
Jes' had to be . . .
An' they wudden one kid there without the same choice.

20

Then down the aisle like an usher came he —
Passin' out things to this 'un and that 'un and even to me.
And it didn't make no difference . . . not even a bit . . .
About who got what, you knew it would fit.
It was jes' like he knowed everybody by name —
Those by the fire . . .
Those in the choir . . .
Passin' out compliments an' praise and hardly no blame.

It was then what Preacher Roland had said 'bout Him,
That little bitty Baby from old Bethlehem,
Jumped in my mind and shone bright and clear.
The likeness of Jesus was now and was here!
You see, the man in red flannel with the white cotton wig —
Odd to think back . . .
Favored Uncle Jack . . .
Did the very same things as that Baby growed big.

He gave of Himself and never took back.
(Thinkin' 'bout it now, it was love in that sack.)
He came in among us and criticized few
And all that He gave us was ever made new.
But the greatest of gifts we'll ever receive —
There are two . . .
For me and for you . . .
Were His death on the cross and His birth on that Eve.

Things I Know

I know a smile I love to see,
   A voice I love to hear;
I know a hand I love to hold,
   A presence I love near;
I know a heart, a loving heart,
   That's thoughtful, fine and true —
I know them all and love them all,
   For they belong to you!

And Mama Baked Bread

Mama Baked Pie
Watercolor

25

An' Mama Baked Bread

Thinkin' back years
Might bring tears,
For memories come back, flood over the soul:
The hard times — the good — those on the dole.
Yet Papa worked long an' never took none,
'Cause "losin' your pride was losin' your fun."
He drove a team to keep us all fed,
— An' Mama baked bread.

Workin' the ground,
Puttin' seed down,
The spring was plantin' and plowin' and such.
Each field knew Papa and his easy light touch.
He truly loved farmin' and watchin' things grow:
Hillside cotton with corn in the field down below.
This man raised his family by sweat an' by wits,
— An' Mama cooked grits.

Worn out tools,
Tired ol' mules,
Weeds grew wild, the beans need a hoe,
Out in the hay meadow Papa would mow.
The summer wore on an' we pray for rain,
For dry-land farmin' leaves an ache and a pain.
We looked for the time of crops laid-by,
— An' Mama fried pie.

Harvestin' time,
Cotton a dime,
But the corn was good and the garden was too,
An' Papa paid the bank as the interest came due.
One more year and we had little to show:
Hand me down clothes, 'cause boys will grow,
Maybe for the oldest there'd be something new,
— An' Mama fixed stew.

Thanksgivin' Day,
Bowin' to pray,
"Thanks for the good crop," was Papa's first thought,
'Cause he'd raised things that couldn't be bought.
For along with the cotton and other such seeds,
He'd planted patience, and kindness, and other good deeds.
"Reap what you sow," he lived by that dream,
— An' Mama froze cream.

Winter was cold,
School got old,
Papa would use those long winter days;
He worked as usual for those were his ways.
But the evenings were special at the family stove:
Radios, games, yarns Grandaddy wove,
An' singing with Grandma like the choirs up above,
— An' Mama served love.

That Feller, Papa, An' Me

"That Feller knowed his stuff!"
Said Papa talkin' there to me.
An' answering back I said, "Yeah,"
'Cause with Papa it's easy to agree.

"That Feller really was a King!"
Said Papa layin' the Bible down.
An' I sorta' caught a glimpse of
Jesus in a crown.

"That Feller was born for man,"
Said Papa kinda' deep in thought.
An' I 'membered the wise men
An' the Baby that they sought.

"That Feller, He helped the poor,"
Said Papa fulla' gratitude.
An' I jes' nodded, "Yes," 'cause
Words might mess the mood.
"That Feller healed the lame!"
Said Papa with a flare.
An' I thought of Freddy's
Limpy leg and said a little prayer.

"That Feller loved the children,"
Said Papa lookin' right at me.
An' I knew that Papa did too . . .
Shoot, that was plain to see.

"That Feller was a happy Man,"
Said Papa startin' in to smile.
An' I jes' grinned a grin to
Show 'im that I had style.

"That Feller, He had troubles too,"
Said Papa quickly addin' more.
An' I had to squinch my eyes to
Keep back a tear or four.

"That Feller was the Son of God!"
Said Papa in a positive way.
An' I felt love a wellin' up,
The kind you can't find words to say.

"That Feller is my kinda' Man,"
Was Papa's reflective view.
An' I found right then . . . that
Papa's views were my views too.

Mules

by Kenneth Wyatt with
apologies to Joyce Kilmer

I think there's nothing quite as cool
As was Papa's big brown mule.
A mule whose scrawny back was bent
From pullin' the wagon where'er we went.

The Mule
Ink Wash

Christmas Dinner

At Grandmama's house on Christmas Day,
Kinfolk they came from miles away.

They was huggin', an' kissin', and greetin' galore.
In would come others an' they'd do it some more.

Gifts were given and happiness shared,
While in the kitchen was dinner prepared.

Then Grandpa would say to bow our head
And close our eyes while the grace was said.

Papa always carved while Mama beamed.
We kids waited — for hours it seemed.

Oh! My eyes were big and my reach was long,
My willpower weak, my hunger strong.

A drumstick — an' maybe a wing!
The pulleybone would make an angel sing!

Pass the bread that Grandma fixed;
I was there to see it mixed.

Some gravy, some cabbage, some black-eyed peas,
A little more mashed potatoes, please.

"Some corn," you say, "before you're thru?"
Well, maybe just an ear or two.

And now for some of Aunt Bum's cake.
That's enough for goodness sake!

I'll tell you this to let you know . . .
There's nothing like it, pure love to show —

When you break bread the Christian way,
It'll make the perfect Christian Day.

To Walk Alone

To walk alone is not my mete,
    Nor is it fair to think it so.
For with my God I linger yet,
    And walk with Him in valleys low.

But yet not always in places deep,
    So up I climb and reach the height
Where Jesus prayed in reverence deep,
    And angels rest from weary flight.

It's peace for us on mountain top
    That care to climb and take it all.
The love of God will never stop,
    And he who takes shall never fall.

The Law
Ink Wash

34

The Ranger

Trouble has always been a part of the West —
From stampedes to card games played close to the vest.
Mix in some tornadoes and grasshopper pest —
Winters could really put a man to the test.
But yet there were days of a far different kind —
And in rode the Ranger with the Law on his mind.

Most troubles can be handled by any cowhand —
From sickness in cows to blow-a-way land.
When calamities came that never were planned,
He just gritted his teeth and showed he had sand.
But sometimes when devils in their lives had done dirt —
Then, in rode the Ranger with a star on his shirt.

Cowboys could survive both flash flood and drought —
Could make his mark known in a fist-a-cuff bout.
He took on widow-makers with never a doubt
And even the horse thieves could usually rout.
But there were killers around that just let it rip —
So, in rode the Ranger with an iron on his hip.

The West needed men like the Ranger that came,
For there were mean men somebody must tame.
He rode not for glory nor money nor fame.
His master was *justice* . . . for all men the same.
So when tough men would throw a loop that was wide,
Right in rode the Ranger . . . with God on his side.

Of God And Love

As man would miss his God . . . so I miss thee.
As a lover would seek his love, I would mine.
For to find thee would my victory be —
For to love thee would make me find.

And to know that I have found what God gave me,
And that love which I found, my life would share,
Made me realize and made me see —
For God in love . . . loves to care.

As God would love his man . . . so I love thee.
As a rich man has his wealth, I have mine.
For to have thee would my riches be —
For to love thee, would make me thine.

To have that love which in thee God did show,
And to know that love will mine always be,
Made me feel and made me know
That the God I love . . . loves me.

Big Bert

The Proposal

Big Bert

Bert, he was a big man, much bigger than most.
"I can lick any man!" was his regular boast.
Broad shoulder . . .
Eyes bolder.

He had walked aside for no man alive;
He jes' took 'em in bunches . . . two, three or five.
Real tough . . .
And rough.

When he was challenged, he said not a whit,
But his neck got red an' he grumbled a bit.
Sheer pride . . .
Somethin' inside.

An' that Saturday night when he came from town,
Jes' stomped in the bunkhouse . . . set hisself down.
He was mad . . .
Kinda' bad.

He jes' stared at the floor and muttered some too,
An' something was said about "nails he could chew."
Couldn't hear . . .
Not clear.

The potbellied stove he kicked down the hall;
He then throwed the cook plumb thru the south wall.
Nobody spoke . . .
Wasn't no joke.

And from that moment on, thangs . . . they got tense;
Bert knocked down the door; he then got the fence.
Outa' his way . . .
Devil to pay.

A rampagin' he went, all over the lot . . .
A grabbin' his pistol, the windmill he shot.
Kicked the cat . . .
Imagine that.

Bellerin' an rantin' he cleared us all out.
He shore was the boss — they jes' wasn't no doubt.
Was quick . . .
No trick.

Not never before had we seen him like that.
He spied me then in the tree where I sat.
Wound tight . . .
Ready to fight.

He stuck up a hand, a wavin' me to come,
"You git you here, boy, there's work to be done."
Couldn't pray . . .
Scared to stay.

"Fetch my white shirt; lay out my black coat."
"What's happenin'?" I whispered, clearin' my throat.
Some change . . .
Little strange.

But the bunkhouse boys knowed what was on
The minute he started a saddlin' that roan.
They knew . . .
So'd you.

"He's off to see Nell," said the boss real low;
"Love's on his mind, sure as winter brings snow."
Saddlin' fast . . .
Gallopin' past.

I took the back road on my little pinto;
By ridin' fast, I'd catch the full show.
Over hills . . .
Rock and rills.

The lights in the house were yellow and pale;
I slipped up close with the darkness a veil.
Listen now . . .
Here somehow.

Big Bert and Nell — they were a standin' outside;
Bert were a talkin' — his hat sweepin' wide.
Voice a tremble . . .
Courage assemble.

"Marryin' you, darlin', is what's on my mind;
I'm awaitin' the answer I hope you can find."
Bated breath . . .
Slow as death.

That Nell had her man was plain and was true,
And in that moment — she whispered, "I do."
All right . . .
Whata' night!

I'm sure there was more that lovers must do,
But I rode away quick to tell all the crew.
Not suprisin' . . .
My apprisin'.

Big Bert was beaten . . . he was tall, but he fell.
'Twas soft moonlight and that sweet Little Nell.
My story . . .
Bert's glory.

Nailed Down
Ink Wash

Nailed Down

"It nails you down," a layman said.
His face should have been crimson red
With shame to speak of churches so.
"When chances come you cannot go
In search of pleasure with your friends,
And all your happy wandering ends.
The things you like you cannot do,
For Christ will make a slave of you."

I looked at him and said, "It's true
That Christ will make a slave of you,
And nail you down with many a blow.
But have you never thought it so
That it's of happiness and pride
That manly Jesus has you tied?
Would you not miss the greater lifts
That come with knowing God's good gifts?"

"It nails you down with nails of care,
And through His church you give and share.
It nails you down with nails so long
That if you're up and feeling strong,
Or yet cast down and all is loss,
They hold secure within the cross.
You cry for 'freedom, time to rest' —
The nailed down slave of Christ is best!"

"Go on your selfish way — and free,
But nailed down . . . I would rather be.
Yes, rather than an earthly crown
I would be, what you say, 'nailed down'.
Nailed down to gentle truths and fair;
Held fast by *Christian* name to wear.
The happiest people in this town . . .
Are those that Christ has fast nailed down!"

The Story Teller

When the work was all done, he'd start it someway —
A casual remark an' jes let it lay.
Then some gullible would up and a 'low
That what he'd said couldn't happen nohow.
Was easy to see he'd hooked him now.
The Storyteller.

He could prove anything with a choice of word —
Occasional truth mixed with absurd.
I can see him now with my memory's eye,
As he sat by the fire while the red embers die . . .
Then cleared his throat to give her a try.
The Storyteller.

Talked about old timers, things that they did —
'Bout the pospectors and the gold that they hid.
He made us believe in snakes that squaredanced;
Showed us the bullet off his buckle that glanced;
The one about black snow kept us fairly entranced.
The Storyteller.

As time marched on, he brought in the ghosts,
And the night sure sudden got darker than most.
He'd brought us full circle from grins to the shakes —
None of us knowin' the real from the fakes,
But for spreadin' it on, he had what it takes.
The Storyteller.

How great it would be just to see him once more,
And hear those tales from his bountiful store.
To laugh at the frog that dreamed he had wings;
To harmonize some with a buzzard that sings,
And gather in words he so easily flings.
The Storyteller.

But the ol' man has gone to the sweet by and by —
Staked out his claim on some star in the sky.
But he's payin' his way, wouldn't take nothing for free,
For I'll bet near a campfire by that quiet crystal sea,
He's telling God's children 'bout a ten-legged flea!
The Storyteller.

The Choice

The days of travel are over.
　The hours of thrill begin
And time and space are to cover
　To yesteryear days of then.

To days of sandals and of story
　O'er roads that seem the same,
We move to scenes of history
　As to the cross He came.

Huge gates of Jerusalem there,
　And on the hill He knelt.
His prayer was prayed from love and care;
　Tears on the ground were felt.

Yet branches slashed, a colt was rid,
　A steadfast face was set—
And care not what Pharisees did,
　Until the future was met.

And it was not to die He came —
　"Let this cup pass!" He prayed.
But death to Christ is not the same—
　It was to LIVE He stayed.

Mother Nature

Mother Nature

I'm always amazed at Mother Nature
    and the way she gets things done . . .
How the flowers can bloom and unfold
    and leaves turn green in the sun.
I'm in wonder at the slow moving sloth
    and how fast the antelope run.
I watch the woolly worm crawl, butterflies fly,
    and the monkeys havin' great fun . . .
From little to big, like the mustard seed,
    or a hippo that weighs 'bout a ton.

She's done a great job in helpin' us all . . .
    She's really done what she oughta'.
She gave a gift to the bird on the wing,
    Chasin' insects till he's caught 'er.
The porcupine quills, the turtle's thick shells—
    Protection there in each quarter.
And if you watch her, you'll see her technique
    Of compensation in order.
Like the man I saw with a very long leg—
    Mother made the other much shorter.

Mother Nature
Oil

Harmonica Music

I never really saw him I confess . . .
Just an old man to ignore I guess.
I strode by him on the board sidewalk
Not even noddin' nor stoppin' to talk . . .
Had no reason, was never inclined.
Now . . . this man is a friend of mine.

It all started when I happened to hear
Notes of a mouth organ soft on my ear.
I paused a step, lookin' round me there;
Quickly saw him tipped up in his chair,
Dressed as he was in his rumpled clothes,
Plain, a cowboy . . . from head to his toes.

Never before had I taken the time,
And stoppin' now had no reason or rhyme,
But hunkerin' down on the chair next door,
I encouraged him then to "play me some more,"
Because hearin' him, I wanted to know
Where those tunes he blew, he learned to blow.

He'd play and he'd talk and led me to see
That all this came from the wide prairie.
When a lad, he rode on big cattle drives,
Movin' toward Abilene where railroads arrive.
And how as he went and marked his way,
He learned for himself harmonica play.

He'd play and we'd talk as the days went free;
Friendship grew with the old man an' me.
Had tales of courage in cowboy life,
Rustlers and fires, struggles and strife,
Of stampedes and dying while working the cows,
And mouth organ music to soothe 'em somehow.

He remembered the boys with talents to spare—
Some were real great . . . yet others, just fair.
One could tell distance right on the dot!
All could do something that others could not.
None could ride like this one kid he knew—
Each had a story . . . every one true.

As he sits there in the sun's golden ray,
I can't help stoppin' when he starts in to play.
To live once again the days on the trail—
The flash floods an lightnin', pelting of hail.
Clear across Texas this Westerner strode . . .
And all the way that harmonica blowed.

The Windmill

Creakin',
Leakin',
Water seekin'.

Millin',
Spillin',
Tank a fillin'.

Turnin',
Churnin',
Praise a earnin'.

Goin',
Blowin',
Life a flowin'.

Aermotor
Ink Wash

Gladness

Can a man buy peace with coin gold—
Or joy sweet for when he's old?
Is peace a time of end of sighs—
And no work . . . tomorrow's prize?
For if this, then, is truth of life,
Lo, for today there's naught but strife.
A question rises chilling cold—
"Where's the gladness of man's soul?"
And stirring deep a spirit tells—
"It's every day that gladness dwells.
And the soul that with gladness shines
Is the soul that gladness finds."

A Christmas Prayer

Nearing Home
Oil

A Christmas Prayer

Evening, Lord, is coming 'cross the sky,
Yet I'm ridin' slow as gates come nigh.
Home's ahead, and hearth and kin are there,
Yet I need time for this Christmas prayer.

You see, Lord . . . Christmas prayers are easy said—
To talk of being spirit and body fed,
Giving thanks for house, and barn, and stall.
It just takes some time to speak it all.

Now, I name the children one by one.
And thank thee, Lord, for the best things done:
All the joys, the laughs, and even tears,
For my wonderful wife of all these years.

I thank Thee, Lord, for the grazing herd,
The circuit rider who preached the word,
The setting sun and the fallen rain,
The rich brown earth of the great high plain.

Bless our friends, Lord . . . please bless 'em grand!
May the Spirit of Christmas cover this land.
Well . . . my prayer's done with my journey's end.
Thanks once more . . . I love Thee, Lord . . . Amen.

The War

I remember one time at the old car shed;
The bumble bees swarmed in the roof overhead.
And me an' my best friend, Pat,
With a cedar-shingle bat,
Went to war to knock 'em all dead.

They would come outa' that hole one by one . . .
Rules were simple, the game would be fun.
Pick out one, and give it a whack!
Standin' there . . . with Pat at my back,
We'd whoop and holler and get it all done.

With backhand an' forehand an' overhead smash
We struck like greased lightning, quick as a flash.
It was easy, easy as pie . . .
Pat could do it a closin' one eye.
If each was nickels, we'd be rollin' in cash.

As time wafted on, we got brazen bold . . .
Two paddles now so we sure had 'em cold.
Pat, you might say, was waxin' it hot . . .
Hit fifty straight, believe it or not.
Our names would be famous when the story was told.

Said my buddy to me, "I got a hunch . . .
A way we can finish this war before lunch."
Pat suggested I hand him a pole,
Said he would kinda' "widen the hole."
With new found freedom, they came in a bunch!

Suddenly we could no longer with ease
Carry the fight to those big bumblebees.
Pat politely got outa' the trail . . .
My runnin' away was askin' to fail.
They chased me and got me from m'head to m'knees.

I awoke two days later just barely alive . . .
Most likely stung by each bee in the hive.
Pat, my friend, was countin' the bumps . . .
Runnin' his fingers down over the humps,
He totaled them up at a hundred and five.

A hundred and five, what a terrible fix—
Bees and wood shingles just never would mix.
Spoke up Pat . . . a wonderful guy,
"How many causes a feller to die?"
I knew, so I answered . . . "One hundred and six!"

Yesterday's Gone

The Dream House

The old house that stood in the country way back
Was the dream of a man who made it a fact.
He came to the land before it was farmed,
Liked the lay of the place, the way it was warmed
By the sun in the winter when the snow was there.
So fixed his mind, he was determined to dare
To take all his money that land to redeem,
And smack in the middle to build there his dream.

He dug deep the foundation a makin' it strong;
Then planned on the outside a porch that was long.
The windows they all reached from ceiling to floor . . .
Hung a big brass knocker on the high front door
That would be tall enough for tallest of men.
He caulked all the cracks to keep out the wind;
Put a pump in the kitchen, stove with a flue;
Each day was one closer to his dream come true.

Each fireplace was brick with damper built in;
The mantles hand carved, ash buckets were tin.
Bedrooms were upstairs all but one for his son.
On the cedar roof when the shinglin' was done
He put up lightning rods to shelter it all.
Hung those modern gas lights to light up the hall.
Then to finish the dream and do it up right,
Bought a glass chandelier with prisms of light.

The vision was finished . . . the years came and went.
Three children grew up and to college were sent;
Bank notes were all paid . . . for the crops were all good;
— Small cracks were now in the white painted wood.
Dreams seemed to fade as the calendar turned;
He didn't rebuild the old barn when it burned.
A few years more . . . the house belongs to the past—
Seems only for dreamers that visions can last.

But I must say this with the story to close,
"A dream never dies . . . but with the dreamer it goes."

Afore The Lamp Was Blowed Out

Remember those nights of
yesterday when the outside
air was a freezin' cold . . .

An' you were a lyin' there
'twixt muslin sheets . . . almost lost
in a featherbed fold?

How you could, as you lay real
still, think over the things that had
happened that day . . .

An' in the same breath claim
all of tomorrow — what you
would do and what you would say?

Listenin' real good, you could hear
from downstairs, your father's footsteps
a stirrin' about . . .

He was, as he should, a doin'
what he could — just afore
the lamp was blowed out.

Remember how cold it was when
you were a kneelin' to say
all your prayers?

But dare not hurry none
'cause Mama's the one
a standin' at the top of the stairs?

Then "God blessin'" everybody
and sayin' "Amen" twice
to get to the close,

You jumped quick into bed with
your feet on a brick to keep from
freezin' your toes?

Next was Mama a walkin' thru
and it's true . . . each
child's bed was sure on her route.

She was sharin' all her love
in that kiss — just afore the
lamp was blowed out.

Remember those nights when
the snow made it quiet with
a blanket of white on the ground . . .

And the flickering lamp made the
shadows dance to the music that
had no sound?

So your mind came alive
to the things in this life
and things in the future to be.

Would you be rich, a doctor
perhaps, or a sailor who put
out to sea?

Could be a cowboy who would
ride on the range, a blacksmith
with muscles and stout.

'Twas important each night just
to be special — just afore the
lamp was blowed out.

Remember it back to your
childhood days and to the home
that kept you from freezin' . . .

Not really with quilts or
even with muslin — but a blanket
of love each season.

Know that love is the flame
that from God's heaven came
just to sit on the soul of man.

And the soul of the home
was the love that we shared
according to God's own plan.

Keep remembering this fact . . .
that love is comin' back when
Christ returns with a shout!

And there are many things
you must do and get done . . .
Afore *your* lamp is blowed out.

Point Of View

The Discussion

Point Of View

"It's lonesome as sin,"
Said one cowboy to the other cowmen.
"Ain't nothing but wind and dirt and grass and rocks.
It's a life of holes in your boots an' holes in your sox.
An' everything you touch has thorns on it.
An' everything you own . . . it never will fit."

"Ain't lonesome at all,"
Said another cowboy to the cowmen all.
"It's a life in a palace — that's certain and shore.
Why, the sky's your ceiling — the ground's your floor.
An' everything in it belongs to you.
An' the only thing that counts is things that you do."

"It's lonesome as sin,"
Said one cowboy to the other cowmen.
"Where nobody knows you and nobody cares;
With nobody to talk to but the cougars and bears.
I tell you, cowboy life is miserable cold.
I tell you, cowboy life is fast gettin' old."

"Ain't lonesome at all,"
Said another cowboy to the cowmen all.
"Everybody's your neighbor; there ain't never no hate.
Dead ahead's a friend if you keep ridin' straight.
I tell you, cowboy life is more'n jes' pay.
I tell you, cowboy life is a glorious way."

"It's lonesome as sin,"
Said one cowboy to the other cowmen.
And jes' reckoned he was tellin' it real,
'Cause livin' out there was a miserable feel.
"Ain't lonesome at all,"
Said another cowboy to the cowmen all.
For he knowed it was all in a point of view,
'Cause livin' out there was livin' life true.

The Card Game

The boys started a gittin' ready
The moment the stage rolled in,
'Cause when they saw that Dude step down,
They counted their money then.
If a fat pigeon had ever lit here,
This one . . . he had feathers on.
Yes sir, the boys, they had an idea . . .
Pluck 'im right down to the bone!

He was a somewhat frailish man
Who wouldn't look eye to eye.
Kinda' nervous and skittish he was;
This would be easy as pie.
The boys were really lickin' their chops
'Bout the money they was due.
Come Satidy night in the ol' back room
They'd drop 'im a lesson or two.

Most likely the game would be poker . . .
A few hands settin' the mood.
One thing for sure not overlooked,
Somebody invited the Dude!
Round the table they sat as one . . .
Grins on the faces of all.
You see, with ol' Dobie a dealin',
They knew how the cards would fall.

The cards fell and the hands went roun' . . .
Now it was time for the deal.
With a new deck and Dobie a shufflin',
This was too good to be real!
The Dude was settin' twixt Curly and Tom . . .
Both of 'em giants of a man.
The cards were dealt jes' five to each,
And ever one picked up his han'.

Startin' to bet . . . they got it real high . . .
But three stayed for the draw.
Tom, he was next to drop out—
Trouble was coming he saw.
The Dude would bet while Curly raised . . .
The limit was reachin' the sky.
The boys were tense, now was the time . . .
Curly was fixin' to try!

Glaring around and cussin' aloud,
Curly was actin' quite rude.
With only one hand he rolled him a smoke,
Right under the nose of the Dude.
With a snap shot he lit up the match,
Held in the hand of Lynn,
Then, squinchin' one eye, he gave it a try . . .
Bettin' it all to win.

The boys could see the pigeon was scared—
His knees were a knockin' fast.
Then takin' a final peek at his cards . . .
He showed 'em the die was cast.
Grabbin' the makings from Curly's chest,
He rolled it circular like . . .
Then with a flourish of confidence,
Threw out a Lucky Strike.

The Dude slapped Tom right outa' his chair,
Grabbin' his gun so fast.
He snapped the trigger of the pistol he stole . . .
Lightin' his smoke by the blast!
Then stackin' his chips on the table of green,
He made 'em pay their dues.
And lookin' straight at Curly, growled,
"Four Aces, boys, you lose!"

Finger Strings

Remind me, Lord, to feed a mouth
And quench a thirst whose lips know drought.
Remind me, too, of those who weep,
And help them, please, my welcome reap.
Remind me, Lord, to clothe those cold
And grasp a hand whose strength is old.
Remind me, please, the sick to find,
And visit prisons of cell and mind.
Remind me, Lord, remind now me—
To do for others — I do for Thee.

The Reminder
Ink Wash

My Son

This day was fast and so was he;
I knew at times there must be three!

You've had in all a mighty day—
A time for dinner, tears, and play.

But now he's still and lids drop low,
A few more nods and dreamin' go.

So rest you now and sleep the night
With visions many of heaven bright:

Of God and Jesus livin' there,
And angel bands with love and care,

Of things to come and bits to do,
The rising sun — a day born new.

Then wake you now to do much more—
Surely, today . . . there must be four!

The New Life

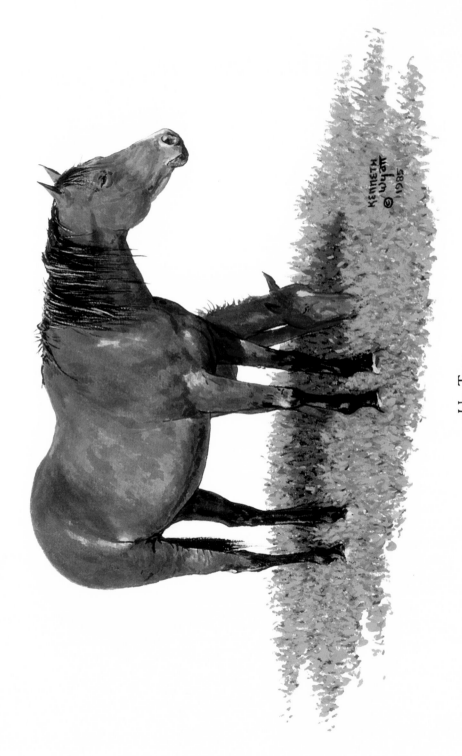

Us Two
Watercolor

The New Life

There are things that get worn or torn.
There are things that are misused, abused,
And we fix and mend and sharpen and straighten,
Take some to the shop with their thirty days waitin'.
The conservatives say, "The old we'll make do,
Sufficient for today; don't go buy anything new."

There are places that we feel fine, sublime!
There are places that we rest, blessed,
And we stay there and live there, and make it our home.
Then we write us a slogan to "never more roam."
The homebodies say to those passin' thru,
"Light down and stay; here's better than anyplace new."

There are people that are real, we feel.
There are people that are fine, we find,
And we open our hearts and take them inside;
Call them our friends with genuine pride.
The clansman would say, "My friends may be few,
But at work or at play, much better than anyone new."

There's a life that we live or give.
There's a life that we take, remake,
And that life is ours — each man to possess.
But the old way won't do — I'm fast to confess.
The Christian would say, "You, lucky you!
Christ's birth and way . . . His very death made everyhing new!"

The Lay Preacher

"Witness", you say? Well now, I don't know.
I'm not much on speaking . . . I think pretty slow.
To stand on the streets and there preach the *word*—
What'll my wife say? . . . She'll think it absurb.
Why people would laugh . . . It'd do me no good.
    Now, don't get me wrong, Lord . . .
      I would if I could.

"Something to give?" Why surely I do!
Name it — you'll have it! I give it to you.
While I'm not wealthy, you can have what I own:
My car and my money and even my home.
Lord, here's my watch . . . my keys and my rings.
    You want what I have?
      Take all of these things.

Or maybe it's time? I've got some to spare.
I'll make out a schedule . . . I'll show you I care:
An hour for church, and one for church school,
An hour to the sick . . . I'll make it a rule.
In service, my Lord, I promise to stay . . .
    Not just a tenth . . .
      I'll give the whole day!

I'll visit the sick, help the poor all to live.
Just anything, Lord . . . I'm ready to give.
It's not that I'm scared . . . it's not that I'm weak . . .
I'm just not ready, not ready to speak.
To call on me now . . . it's really not fair.
    I need some time . . .
      Got lots to prepare.

What did you say? Let's hear that again.
"Time's running out! There's souls yet to win!"
Yes, I know that Lord, but what good am I?
I've got some good thoughts, but in words they just die.
You say you'll be with me when I stand up to speak . . .
    Not just on Sunday . . .
        But all through the week?

Well . . . now I'd like it . . . I've gotta' confess.
If I just thought I could, I'd have to say **yes**!
Just trust in your word, believe that I can?
"Like a mustard seed," Lord? Yes, I understand.
And I'll do it, too, Lord — You wait an' don't fear.
    I'll preach about Jesus . . .
        So others can hear.

Finished
Ink Wash

78

Growin'

"Stand by the wall,"
Mother would call,
And then mark with her pencil on top of your head.
That would show
How you grow,
And the lines on the door left you taller instead.

Like boys and girls,
All things unfurl
As they grow and stretch and then push for more room.
And we say,
"That's the way
God is weaving each life in this earth on his loom."

Growing's His plan
You understand,
For only things growing can continue to live.
True of you
And me too,
For this life requires that we grow ere she give.

Don't be misled;
Learn this instead:
To stop growing is deadly, so this must be told.
Hear it now,
Heed somehow—
We will grow in most ways, but we never GROW old.

The Christmas Stocking

Can be red or green or even striped;
Can be plain, fancy or even lacy piped.
Long, short, maybe somewhere in betwixt,
New or even old with a gapin' hole to fix,
Big or little, even thick or thin,
Christmas Eve, I hung it where it should a been.

> I'm talkin' 'bout the Christmas stocking
> I hung at Christmas time.
> An' thought I'd tell you 'bout rememberin' it
> With this here bit of rhyme.

Some were knitted and very neatly seamed.
(I've used 'em dirty but mostly recent cleaned.)
A few were silk with double toe and heel,
Others cotton, soft to touch and feel.
One was wool . . . sheared right off the sheep,
Kinda' itchy, but really long and deep.

> I'm talkin' 'bout the Christmas stocking
> On which my hopes were pinned,
> And 'bout my prayers that night—
> Cleanin' up the sins I'd sinned.

I'd spend the night in Papa's ol' chair;
Early next morning I had to be there!
With loving care, yet eagerness too,
I dug right in and searched it thru.
Laid it out in a perfect row;
Couldn't quit 'til I reached the toe.

> I'm talkin' 'bout the Christmas stocking
> That I turned inside out,
> And 'bout each new treasure
> That brought a squeal or shout.

Oh there wuz apples and nuts for sure;
Candy enough for a sweet tooth cure . . .
It was gumdrop, cane, and ribbon too,
And in between, a chocolate or two.
A yellow banana, an orange so round,
In among 'em, some presents were found.

I'm talkin' 'bout the Christmas stocking
Nailed to the mantle above . . .
Packed tight with goodies,
Yet . . . stuffed with love.

Of Things Broken
Ink Wash

Of Things Broken

Shall we hide it from sight . . .
Tongue about it be quiet . . .
Those things ragged and tattered and torn and broken?
Must need all things be new . . .
Will the old never do . . .
Not to mend, but broken things just remain broken?

"Little value," you say.
"Not in this age and day
For these things are unsightly and useless to me."
But don't say it at all . . .
Not in soul be so small . . .
For many yesteryear things were broken for thee.

See four men as they come . . .
They carry the sick one . . .
And the crowd swells and presses and pushes the line.
So to the roof they take . . .
With the hand they did break . . .
And I know deep inside that their faith could be mine.

In the midst of the storm . . .
The wind in fury form . . .
Took with tossing and pitching the vessel apart.
And fast to broken things
A drowning Paul clings
To live on and write words for the heart.

To height of the mountain . . .
With words of the Fountain,
He taught them of blessings, so they might know.
Fingers touched bread;
Thousands were fed!
The breaking of crust gave eternal-life flow.

Look not down but up . . .
To the cross from a cup . . .
And the shouting and leering and jeering of men.
A body is broken . . .
No word to be spoken . . .
For the act in itself is for now as for then.

Hence remember and know . . .
God does not for show . . .
And things ragged and tattered and tearing and breaking
Give knowledge that God takes
Anything that man breaks,
And with wisdom and love . . . He something better is making.

You Are Mine

I am glad you are mine for I am
   changed when I am with you.
My soul, my life, my thoughts are
   moved by what you do.
And it's not just doing, for everyone
   "does" in his own way,
It's bringing out of me that which
   needs brought out each day.
The reaching of your heart into my
   heart, and then content,
The winking at ignorant things I've
   done and not meant.
The pulling out of creative luggage
   that within me be,
Yet, no one save you had ever
   probed to see.
So reaffirm my vows and plight
   again my troth to you,
For God gave thee me, and since—
   my life was new.

Mama's Quilt
Ink Wash

The Quilting

Do words like binding or blocking
   mean something to you?
Or rolling or marking or the word
   coverlet too?

Because if'n they do, and you might
   recognize some,
You probably remember how
   yesterday's woman had fun.

They regular would gather in a
   close neighborly way,
Startin' in about noon for the
   rest of the day.

With huggin' and kissin', sweet
   greeting they shares,
Then set up the quilt frame
   on the dining room chairs.

Now matching the colors they careful
   threaded the eye . . .
(Grandmother always got it on
   the very first try.)

And their fingers were nimble . . .
   how fast they could quilt!
With fine, tiny stitches,
   the patterns were built.

It might be a hexagon or a
   gold appliqué,
One called *Sun Bonnet Baby* or
   The Flower Garden gay.

No matter the pattern, they could be
    crazy or patched,
The day moved on smoothly as
    the stitches they matched.

And the goal in their mind was
    not "tackin' out;"
It was the love they were sharing
    and talkin' about.

You see, when they all left there, the
    binding complete,
In true friendship the next time, they were
    ready to meet.

Mama Liked The Wildflowers

Chapel At Blue Hill

Mama Liked The Wildflowers

In back of the house where the pasture lay,
After winter was gone and warm was the day,
The bright new flowers came a pushin' up . . .
The pairie phlox and the buttercup.
Mama walked there . . .
In the clean spring air.
'Cause Mama . . . she liked the wildflowers.

Daddy grew roses and knew every one;
Max took mornin' glories, facin' the sun;
Sis favored honeysuckle, smellin' so sweet;
Plain ol' zinnias was the choice of Pete;
Runnin' trumpet vine
Was always mine,
But Mama . . . she liked the wildflowers.

She planted others an' got 'em to grow:
Daisies and marigolds standin' in row,
Petunias in beds, hollyhocks in hills,
Had some violets on the kitchen sills.
Were pretty too—
But we all knew . . .
Best, Mama . . . she liked the wildflowers.

She'd gather them in and press 'em in books,
Learn their names and know 'em by looks:
The Meadow Pink and the Butterfly Weed,
A tall Star Thistle with its pockets of seed,
The Storkbill,
Yellow Flutter Mill.
Yes, Mama . . . she liked the wildflowers.

And if we younguns might misbehave
Or disobey orders that Daddy gave,
Took from her bed the three center slats,
Maybe turpentined the barnyard cats . . .
Always we'd trust-
Even when she fussed,
That Mama liked us . . . her **wildflowers.**

The Saddle
Ink Wash

The Pinto Pony
And The Silver Saddle

Back yonder when I was ten and my sister was six,
I found myself in somewhat of a fix.
   It was Christmas Eve and out on the snow
   Santa was lost; he wouldn't show.
At least that's the story that Daddy had spread
When we knelt that night in prayer by the bed.

It was a restless time as I turned and tossed,
Afraid my dream most certainly was lost.
   A dream that began with a letter I wrote,
   Not 'xactly a letter, more of a note.
An' then the postman mailed it to Santa to see,
So he'd know what presents I was wantin' for me.

Seldom in December that Texas weather hits hard,
But the norther came; snow covered the yard.
   The reindeer couldn't fly; they couldn't see.
   Gifts wouldn't come, obvious to me.
Yet Mama smiled, tuckin' the quilt that night,
And promised the morning would dawn clean bright.

Let me tell you what happened while Sis and I slept.
The clouds slid away; guess the angels had helped.
   A sleigh had been by, leavin' its tracks,
   An' standin' outside, I'm givin' you facts,
Was a dream come true for us boys that chase cattle-
A black and white pinto and a small silver saddle.

The Steel Bronco

It ain't easy to admit, that's sure enuff,
A life time 'uv knowledge and such-like stuff,
'Cause, podner, it's this I want you to see . . .
Jes' want to show how ignorant I be.

Wuz on Friday the 12th that nightmare begin . . .
That Englishman ridin' his buckskin 'uv tin.
On dust clouds boilin', he came down the road . . .
The horses they scattered and shucked ever' load.

He went with a roar, a shout and a scream—
The roar from the motor that drank gasoline,
The herd ran off in directions of three—
The shout was from him . . . the scream came from me.

For some get jolted from lightnin' on high,
And some get shot as at poker they try.
But I wanta' say Death's sickle I feels
The minute I seen that mustang on wheels.

Had horns like a steer with a saddle built in;
Wheels it had on north and south end.
Jes' one glass eye that rode in the center . . .
Was all in all, a miserable critter.

"Motorcycle," he said, explainin' it so,
"Grab holt of her horn - get on and go!"
And this I'll say, "If it's ridin' you crave—,
Straddle her only . . . the bold and the brave."

With the gauntlet flang down, cowboys go wild . . .
Right in the middle two 'uv us piled.
Ol' Sam on back and me in front,
Our legs almost drug . . . this hoss was a runt.

Thangs happened fast when I twisted one horn;
I 'most repented the day I was born.
Grabbed fer the horn and jes' got a honk,
And Sam with his hat was fannin' that bronc.

We screamed like Injuns and went straight ahead;
In the back of my mind arose a big dread.
"The river's down thar," I shouted to Sam,
And I yelled "Haw!" and "Gee!" to turn it around.

But listen it wouldn't, not even at "Whoa!"
So then with the spurs I give it a go.
In the flanks I shot 'em, got 'em in deep,
No horseflesh I hit, but spokes quite a heap.

With chain on my leg and Sam on my back,
Deep in the river we made a neat stack.
Now some horses comes, and some horses goes,
But round that steel pinto the river still flows.

I'm warnin' you long; I'm warnin' you loud.
If interested only in wearin' a shroud,
Get a Steel Bronco and throw up a leg,
But remember my story . . . I most humbly beg.

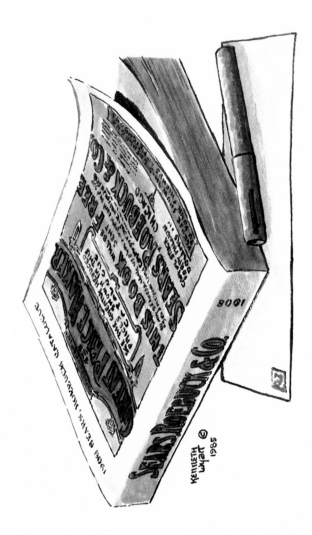

Sears and Roebuck
Ink Wash

The Wishbook

When Daddy brought it in,
No one could figure just where he'd been
To locate such a book
Designed for all to look.
And for hours he let us kinda' ponder,
Then told us that, "In town back yonder
Was a store in which you did not wander
But from this book you took."

Sears an' Roebuck was the name
And selling mercantile was their game.
All you ever had to do,
If you needed somethin' new,
Why, say like a brand new button hook,
A whatnot shelf for a corner nook,
Was to turn the pages of this book
And order one or two.

Came equipped with order sheet.
You just wrote the item numbers neat,
Then dropped it in the mail,
Guaranteed it would not fail.
Next, settle back for a week or two,
Just let the catalogue do its do . . .
Watch that order come back to you.
Sears had made another sale!

And it never mattered none.
If was wanted, you could order one:
A trap to catch a fox,
A new pair of woolen sox,
A gingham dress to a garden tool,
Carpenter square or a measurin' rule.
Turn the page, and dress your mule!
It came right to the box.

The pleasures that it gave,
As over its many pages did we rave,
Have lasted all my way.
And in my mind there lay
Many visions that I can conjure out
Since at first my father I did doubt
That things could be bought on a rural route . . .
The Sears and Roebuck way.

Doctorin'

"Won't hurt much," was Daddy's low sigh
When with his knife he began to pry,
And pulled out the splinter with care
The old wooden fence had slivered in there.
An' then when I saw that it was all done,
That he had healed his most favorite son,
The thought came to me an' lingers there yet—
He could have been a doctor, I bet.

"Don't be a baby!" my uncle cajoled—
His exasperation just hardly controlled,
And shoved out the spoon full to the brim.
He looked at me an' I looked at him,
Then closin' my eyes plus holdin' my breath,
I swallered it down near chokin' to death.
Doctorin' for him was castor oil pure
And work it did . . . for certain and sure.

"You'll be better soon!" said Mother with love
As she stood by the bed kinda' hoverin' above.
Drops in my nose, puttin' Vicks on my chest,
Tellin' me then, "Please get you some rest,"
And squeezin' a lemon and makin' a mug
Of hot lemonade she served with a hug.
Angel of mercy . . . both doctor and nurse—
That was Mama when we children got worse.

Oh, daddies are fine and uncles are too;
There're some ailments they can pull you right thru.
An' mothers, I tell you, just can't be beat
For puttin' a feller right back on his feet.
But there are times when things get too rough,
And home doctorin' is just not enough.
Then Pa would hitch up and head out for town
To fetch the doctor and have him come round.
An' he never was called 'cept that he went—
That ol' Country Doctor was pure Heaven sent.

About Grandmothers

Grandmothers can
    Make a rainy day go fast;
    Make candy that cannot last;
    Hug you so you cannot breathe;
    Love you so you cannot leave.

Grandmothers will
    Send you cards of colors bright;
    Tell you stories half the night;
    Forget the naughty things you do;
    Remember all the birthdays too.

Grandmothers seem
    So pretty — just every day;
    So kind — just in every way . . .
    And sweet — why honey's sour,
    And nice — better by the hour.

Grandmothers are
    Like angels come down to men;
    Like Christmas when you were ten;
    Like heaven — why all the time.
    "Whose?" you say. Why yours . . . and mine!

Grandmother
Ink Wash

When Daddy Reached
The Bible Down

With supper et an' th' dishes all dried,
Fire banked and the damper tried,
The milkin' done an' strained an' such,
Beds turned down with Mother's touch . . .
Then Daddy reached the Bible down.

Position his chair an' motion us near—
Gittin' close the better to hear.
He'd check the coal oil an' trim the light,
End of day an' startin' of night . . .
Then Daddy reached the Bible down.

Breathe on his glasses an' polish 'em good,
Clear his throat like we knew he would.
Then gentle an' soft as a lovin' look
Those work-hard hands opened the Book . . .
When Daddy reached the Bible down.

To turn the page, he'd lick his thumb wet,
Look over his glasses, get everything set.
Then in a voice that sounded some like Love,
He read 'bout Christ sent from above . . .
When Daddy reached the Bible down.

In the summer months he read about good
Carpenter Jesus: where he stood,
Sermons he preached, the miracles done,
Read the parables one by one . . .
When Daddy reached the Bible down.

Come fall an' Daddy thumbed to John;
Read about *Love* th' perfect bond.
"Love one another," he'd gravely say,
Then wink at Ma his special way . . .
When Daddy reached the Bible down.

Middle of winter brung a special part
"Bout the baby Child," strong of heart,
And Mary his mother, the wise men three.
Readin's a pleasure near a Christmas tree . . .
When Daddy reached the Bible down.

Resurrection part that came in spring
Made more sense than anything.
'Cause with God all things are new through Him
Like these memories by lamplight dim . . .
When Daddy reached the Bible down.

A Pair of Lamps
Ink Wash

The Coal Oil Lamp

Take you down that lamp of brass,
Polish bright the globe of glass—
(Newspaper wad does the trick)
Fill 'er up . . . then trim the wick.
Now settle in for come what may,
And the coal oil lamp closed the day.

There were things that happened by a coal oil light
That just wouldn't work in the broad daylight.
So while you're a sittin' and listenin' real good,
I'll stir up some memories of an early childhood.

Cornbread an' beans was supper fare,
An' Mama's cobbler a settin' there,
Sweet, cold milk from the cooler tray,
Papa's deep voice when bowin' to pray.
Seven o'clock an' all's all right
When the coal oil lamp started the night.

You can speak right up and say what you say,
About startin' the night and closin' the day;
But I'll take kerosene by match to be lit,
As round the oak table the family would sit.

Business talked while dishes were dried,
Kids waited patient . . . fit to be tied,
Apron hung up, Mama came near,
Grandpa scooted up . . . better to hear,
Papa chuckled . . . his face was a grin.
By coal oil light the show would begin.

Papa was a showman with Mama at his knee,
Plus there was Grandma, Grandpa an' children all three.
And there in the dimness of that farmhouse so small,
Papa played actor, an' preacher, an' teacher for all.

Magic there was with coins that fly,
Handkerchiefs jumped . . . we didn't know why,
Laughin' long at stories he told,
Sides hurting . . . they never got old.
Mama sat there a gigglin' low . . .
Coal oil lamp had her face all aglow.

Brother recited poetry from school that day;
Grandpa on special occasions his fiddle would play.
Strange as it seems and us not knowin' how,
Everybody was up and a takin' a bow.

Sister would sing, I told a joke,
Suddenly Grandma quietly spoke . . .
Ghost stories by a lamplight flame,
Shadows alive . . . nothing's the same.
Papa's big laugh made it all right.
Evenings went fast by coal oil light.

Then finally at last the big Bible was read,
And that lamp light readin' gets you ready for bed.
So tucked away all, we'd sleep thru the night,
And Papa reached over . . . and turned down the light.

The Yeller Dog

Buddies
Watercolor

The Yeller Dog

Uncle Jake came to the party when I was a pup,
Rode to the house and came walkin' right up.
Warn't really invited — you didn't do it that way;
Jake was his own man . . . he'd go or he'd stay.

I'd only seen him 'bout twice once before,
But I knowed him sure when he walked in the door.
Stood six foot three inches and my name sake;
Why, "Little Jake" was written right there on the cake.

"I heared you was growed up," he said with a grin;
I showed him the candles to prove I was ten.
"I figured you was and decided to call —
Feel here in the pocket of my old mackinaw."

Well, excited I was and you'd been too,
If Uncle Jake had brung somethin' to you.
I run my hand down in the pocket quite deep;
My fingers felt there what I was willin' to keep.

So I laid holt on and drug it right up,
And showed to the world a bright yeller pup.
When I seen that dog, I jes' lost my heart!
Uncle Jake allowed, "You never will part."

Well, the party got over and time moved along.
In those nine years many things has gone wrong:
Uncle Jake moved away and Mama, she died,
And Pa never got over it . . . as hard as he tried.

Droughts we had, a war came and went,
Did some soldierin' for our government.
Yet with me each year, both summer and fall,
Was that gift from the pocket of a big mackinaw.

We played and worked through the years as we growed —
The most faithful companion that man ever knowed.
And things can be handled if you're lucky, you see —
Luck comes in pairs . . . a yeller dog and me.

Signs

Now there's a word for you—
    That word spelled . . . S-I-G-N.
Let me explain what I think, and
    This is how I'll begin.
That word will mean nearly anything
    You want it to say.
You can just speak it out real easy
    And then let it there lay.

                like . . .

"It's sure a *sign* of true manhood," says
    A father to son,
As with a razor in hand his first
    Shave he's begun.
"That's a *sign* of wickedness!"
    The preacher Sunday did shout,
And that's another way of
    Kickin' ol' Satan about.

                or . . .

It's a *sign* of old age
    When we first begin to forget,
But we're all headed there, it's
    For certain, you bet.

                or . . .

"You must bear to the left," it will
    Read black on the white.
It's a *sign* by the highway that
    Makes your left turn right.

                or . . .

"It's a *sign* of the times," says
    The broadcaster of news.
Then, with that statement out front,
    We settle for half truths.

                or . . .

"*Sign* up today!" says Uncle Sam
    On the poster outside.
It's a *sign* saying "*sign*" — touched with
    National pride.

or . . .

"Is Virgo your *sign*?" inquires
   The astrologer wit;
She's hoping of course her predictions
   Will fit.

or . . .

"That's a sure *sign* of love," coos the
   Mother to girl
While believing inside it's a
   Fanciful whirl.

or . . .

"*Sign* on the line," confers
   The pompous banker to me,
"Why the note will be paid when you reach
   A hundred an' three."

or . . .

Be proud of your work, and put
   Your name on it too,
Signin' it shows you're some pleased
   What you do.

or . . .

"I'm signin' off; Rubber Duck is 10-4
   An' down."
An' the truck driver's gone from the
   Radio sound.

or . . .

"Thar's Injun *sign* a plenty," says
   The scout to the boss;
His a readin' that *sign* careful has
   Prevented hair loss.

You see . . .

There are *signs* that are dim;
   There are *signs* that are bright;
There are *signs* that are dreadful;
   There are *signs* that are right.

It's . . .

"Sign up!" "Sign in!" "Sign out!" "Sign off!"
   You can see what I say—
But remember . . . your heedin' those *signs*
   Jes' might show THE WAY.

The Full Circle

The baby's head looked like this
   at the start.
Not really much hair . . . not
   enough for a part.

A little bit older, and then
   it did grow.
At the age of ten
   over the ears it did flow.

But the girls he did notice
   reaching the teens.
Now it's not bushed, but
   with oil it gleams.

In college with him
   the ladies went wild.
His hair was coiffuered!
   He wore it in style.

Then youth did go and with
   it, his hair.
Suddenly on top was nothing
   but bare.

Jes' look at him now
   not wearin' his hat . . .
He's right back where
   he started at.

Home On Time

Down The Trail

Home On Time

There's a miracle that I've known since I was a boy.
   Oh, it's not your regular kind of loaves and fishes,
   Or even modern ones of answers to wishes.
     But it's miraculous still . . .
     And iffen' you will,
Let's all think together on this here most wonderful joy.
     That miracle divine . . .
     How daddies always seem to get home on time.

It's on particular days that this miracle is bright,
   Say like Halloween, graduations, and weddin' the bride.
   To be where he should was a part of his pride.
     He found the right place . . .
     A grin on his face.
Many hours he had traveled — all day and all night.
     The miracle divine . . .
     How daddies always seem to get home on time.

It was his job that kept him gone to a faraway crew.
   And it wasn't as if that he didn't care,
   But you *knew* on Easter — he wouldn't be there.
     Then, man among men . . .
     He did it again.
Made it back, hid the eggs, got to church on the pew.
     That miracle divine . . .
     How daddies always seem to get home on time.

And it worked on birthdays, Thanksgiving and the 4th of July.
   No matter the miles that lay in the way,
   Or even the weather — how late in the day.
     Give him a reason . . .
     Any ol' season.
Why, it was like nothing — like done on the sly!
     That miracle divine . . .
     How daddies always seem to get home on time.

Yearly, it was Christmas that gave us a fright.
  That he gave the most presents rightly was true;
  Why, even when broke he managed a few.
    And what if it snowed? . . .
    Mama, she knowed.
So, she kept the light burning on that cold winter night.
    That miracle divine . . .
    How daddies always seem to get home on time.

EPILOGUE

Now we're all grown and have kids of our own,
  And it's us that goes those very long miles
  To the ol' home place and Mama's quiet smiles.
    Was not really the same . . .
    But the miracle came
To heal up our hearts now that Daddy's gone on
    To Heaven sublime . . .
    For Daddy always was one to get home on time.

Talkin' To The Boss

Many's the time on a Christmas Eve night,
With snow piled high and the stars turned bright,
Papa would saddle ol' Half-pint late,
Gather the reins and ride thru the gate.

He'd ride north to his favorite place,
Tug off his hat and bow down his face,
Then with only God and the stars up there,
He'd always pray his favorite prayer.

Papa prayed with a heart full of love,
Praisin' the Christ Child and the Father above.
He prayed out loud and prayed silent too,
Jes' prayed and prayed — until he was thru.

Sometimes he'd stay for a full hour long,
Then come ridin' back a bubblin' with song.
'Course we never knew what all he'd say,
But we all knowed he knew how to pray.

And later on as we sat round the tree,
Mama beside and me on his knee,
We found our not goin' wasn't no loss
'Cause then and there we shared his
        TALK TO THE BOSS.

School Days

School days
Learning pays

Brother went
Mostly sent

Wouldn't learn
Teacher stern

"Study, boy!"
"Brain employ."

Brother dumb
Unlike some

Couldn't cry
Wouldn't try

Failing way
Doesn't pay

Daddy knew
Waited too

Flailed away
Half-a-day

Paddle burned
Brother learned!

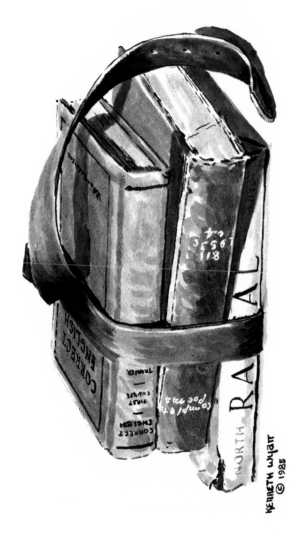

School Days
Ink Wash

The Circuit Rider

A man he was, don't doubt you none,
Plumb clean thru, foot to head.
And not just size nor deeds he'd done,
Most was the things he'd said.

Ah, big he was with a lop-side smile,
And gentle, too, you bet.
Ask him — he'd go that extra mile;
A stranger never met.

"He's from south Texas," Papa believed.
"Comes 'bout twice a year.
Joy comes with him and when he leaves,
The womens sheds a tear."

A claw-hammer coat, a black felt hat,
Boots run down at the heel,
Proud on a tall bay horse he sat,
The Leather Book was real.

The Reverend, that was Mama's choice,
Preacher to all us rest.
But names didn't matter — just the voice
When certain you'd be blest.

Then singin' he was at a fearsome pace;
The power of God was near.
That circuit rider led us to grace
An' love shoved out the fear.

Sudden he'd open the Book leather bound.
Holy was the word come true!
The birth, the death, then life all around,
Jesus' life plumb thru!

Glory came down and flooded the place;
Religion was right as rain.
You could see God's peace on every face;
Pardon washed every stain.

That man of the cloth could do it all—
Touched every child and man.
Listen close . . . you'd hear the angel's call
From thrones in the promised land.

Then, baptizing done, and scripture all taught,
Plus I guess marryin' a few,
The rider rode on, leavin' one last thought . . .
That "God loves 'specially you!"

Once A Day And Twice On Sunday

As I remember Papa, and he was grand,
He was head of the house, a man of the land.
A right righteous self, yet God fearin' too,
Kept stock of his blessings his whole life thru—
Once a day
And twice on Sunday.

Respected alike by his neighbor and kin;
To of trusted him once was to trust him ag'in.
"His word is his bond," and that was said true,
For with honor and love he touched those he knew—
And that was ever' day
And twice on Sunday.

A real cowman he was, but that came late,
Right after Mama and God and children, all eight.
Was a real smart man in spite of no school,
Jes' common good sense and a bright Golden Rule—
Followed ever' day
And twice on Sunday.

Our mama, she was special in this man's life.
"Precious she is," Papa said of his wife.
He'd look in her eyes and hug her real slow,
And speak of love kinda' easy and low —
At least once a day
And twice on Sunday.

About the kids Papa thought quite a lot,
From the oldest brother to the littlest tot.
He taught us the good an' raised us up well,
Kept a holdin' us up ever' time we near fell—
Anytime a day
And twice on Sunday.

To the girls he was soft and easy to sway.
(They was jes' like Mama, they had their own way)
How they could use him, great heavens above!
To them he was Daddy, to him they wuz love —
Usually ever' day
And twice on Sunday.

When all we boys would swagger an' talk mean,
It would really hurt his heart at what he'd just seen.
So he'd shed a tear, but then set his jaw,
'Cause he knew in our house, his word must be law—
All day ever' day
And twice on Sunday.

And thinkin' back, as I remember it now,
The rod wasn't spared, but we were somehow.
For guessin' the reason, we all made it grown.
It was Papa's religion for which he was known—
Always ever' day
And twice on Sunday.

You see, he had faith and could spread it around.
Find a problem too hard and his knee would touch ground.
The time and the place, it meant nothing at all
For there in his faith on his knees he stood tall—
Eventually once a day
And twice on Sunday.

In Papa we all knew that God had a man,
Whether standin' in church or kneelin' in sand.
Truth is, God is God wherever he'd go.
It was prayin' that did it, we know it was so—
Once a day
And twice on Sunday.